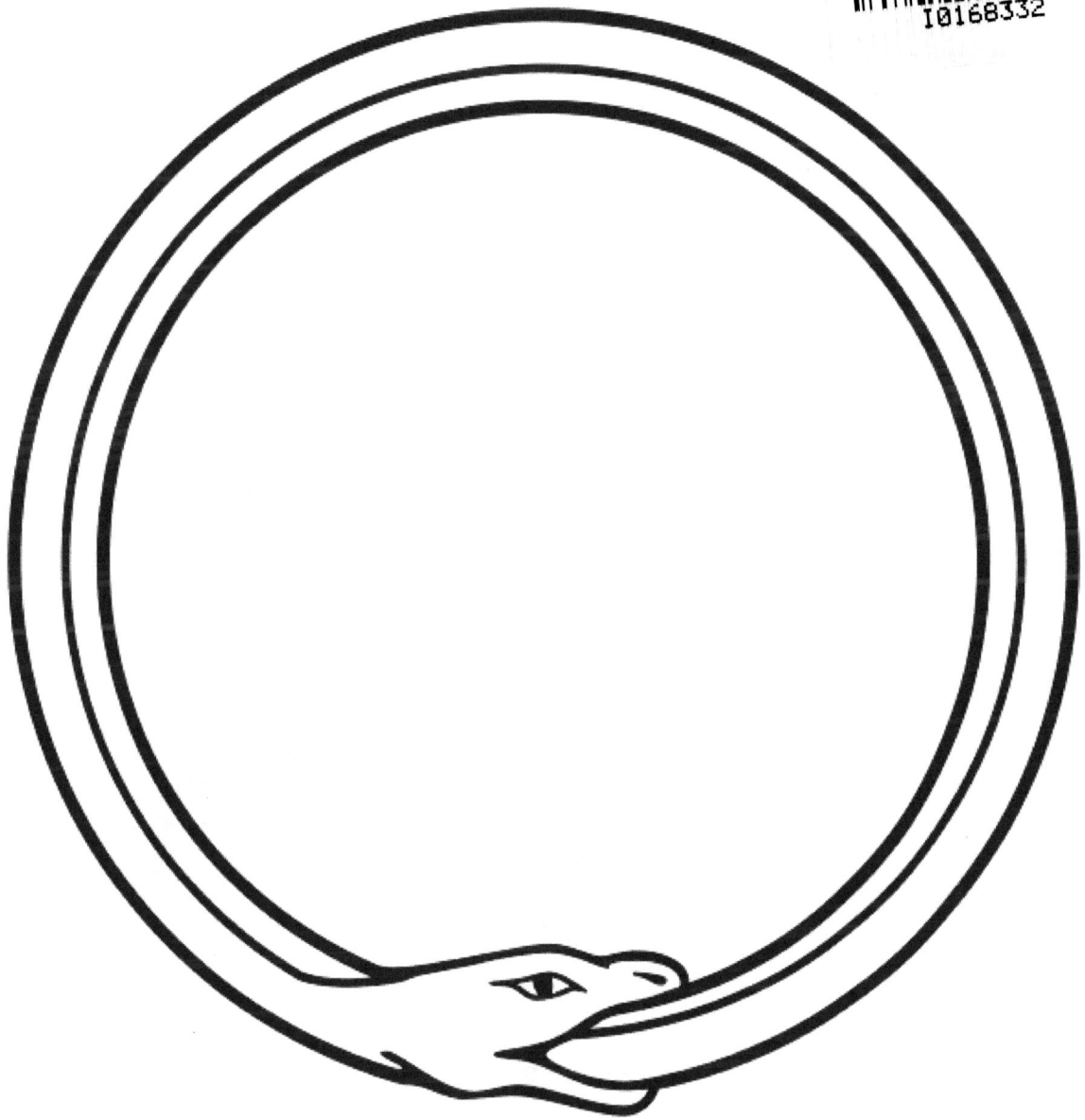

Other NY Quarterly books by Richard Kostelanetz

Recircuits (2009)

Three Poems (2011)

Works of poetry by Richard Kostelanetz in other media -

Echo (Silkscreened paper, 1975)

Word Prints (Silkscreened paper, 1976)

Milestones in a Life (Poster, Pittsburgh Poetry on the Buses, 1980)

Antitheses (Hologram, 1985)

Stringtwo (Inkjet print 200' long, 2004)

Warm/Cold (Acetate print, 2004)

Reimagining Rockaway Postcards (Paper prints, 2004)

The East Village (Paper prints, 2004)

Black Writings (Inkjet prints, 2010)

Shorter Ouroboros (Jars, 2011)

Art (Acetate print, 2013)

OUROBOROS

RICHARD KOSTELANETZ

NᵈQ Books™

The New York Quarterly Foundation, Inc.
New York, New York

NYQ Books™ is an imprint of The New York Quarterly Foundation, Inc.

The New York Quarterly Foundation, Inc.
P. O. Box 2015
Old Chelsea Station
New York, NY 10113

www.nyq.org

First Edition

Set in Wide Latin

Layout and Design by John Also Bennett

Author Photo by Nona Eleanor Ellis

Library of Congress Control Number: 2014941160

ISBN: 978-1-63045-009-0

For Ferdinand Kriwet, who discovered circular writing before me.

From the beginning of my work in visual poetry forty-five years ago, I wanted to create from words alone images so strong that they would stick in viewers' heads long after their eyes turned away from my work. When I first heard the epithet afterimage as an honorific among visual artists, I recognized it as analogous to the strongest lines in strictly verbal poetry. Now that I've seen others claim the epithet Visual Poetry for words embedded in other kinds of images (usually less distinguished), I feel more reason to declare and extend my original ambition that I find that with words alone I can make the most powerful afterimage available to me.

Richard Kostelanetz
FarEast BushWick, NY, 11385-5751
14 May 2014

INSURGENT

1

ESPERANTO

2

3

HERAION

4

ANTITHESIS

BENTOMOM

6

ENTHUSIASM

GO UTI A M IN

8

I C E S O Y E R R

9

TESTAFE

AESTHETICALLY

SIGNATURE

ARCHETYPE

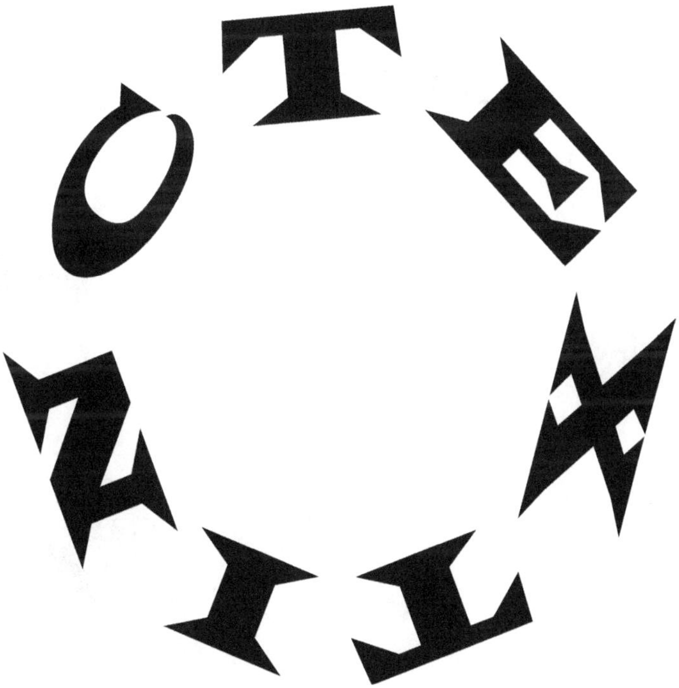

TEAPPEIT

16

INCANDESCENT

OUTSHEREABO

I C A N E M

MANTAGONISM

ADOLESCENT

21

COLLECTION

DECOR OR

INTERSECT

FRATEAMILIO

25

DISABLED

SLUMINOUSD

ETOUCHSTONE

28

USOLEAGINOU

29

DORSEN

EAT AT TEN ATE

EARLIEST

DEANTIPODE

33

REDUCATOR

34

LISEEMBELT

36

HENGLIS

38

STARS IN O

40

ENLARGEMENT

41

SEXPERISE

42

INFINITIES

GIRDLE

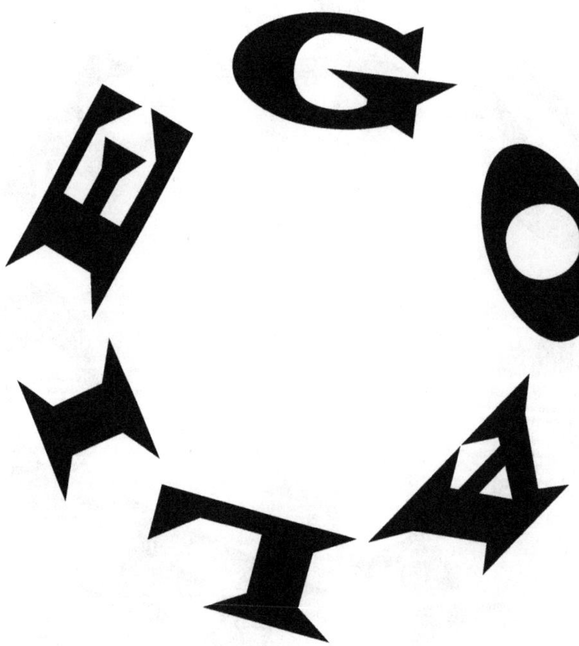
G O A T I E

RHEA GONORRHEA ONO

HALITOSIS

DOUTHAND

50

T H E N O C E O F E H T R O

HELPLESS

52

ILLUSTRIOUS

PRIMPROPER

CHINA SMUD

RESTE VED O D O

56

U M I N D E O C O R

THUMPENT

PHENOMENA

ULTIMATUM

REINSPIRE

62

LORD BAY

WITHOUT GROWTH

INTEGUMENT

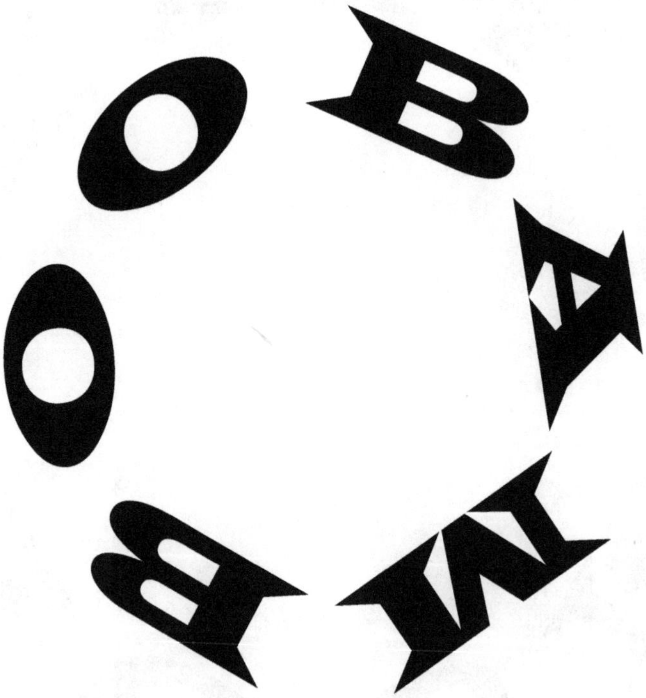

ALINTESTINA

CHARMONIC

MANDRIN

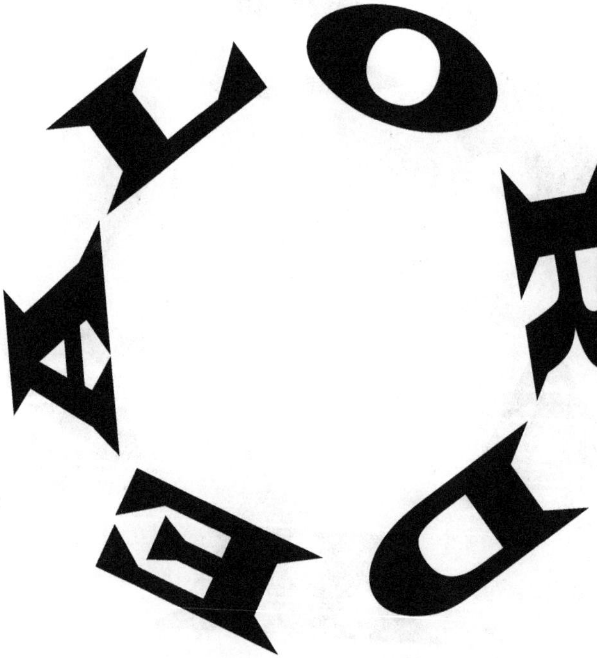
ORDEAL

71

U S E M E N E O P A

72

GEMASSE

ORGY METAL

74

ETERM

USNONOTORIOUS

POSTLEAP

PERORATOR

ENTRANTS

81

UTOPIENT

ESTABILIZE

83

84

OUTERMOST

85

ARTIST ICARTIS

E R O U C S I D E

88

HEARD OVER

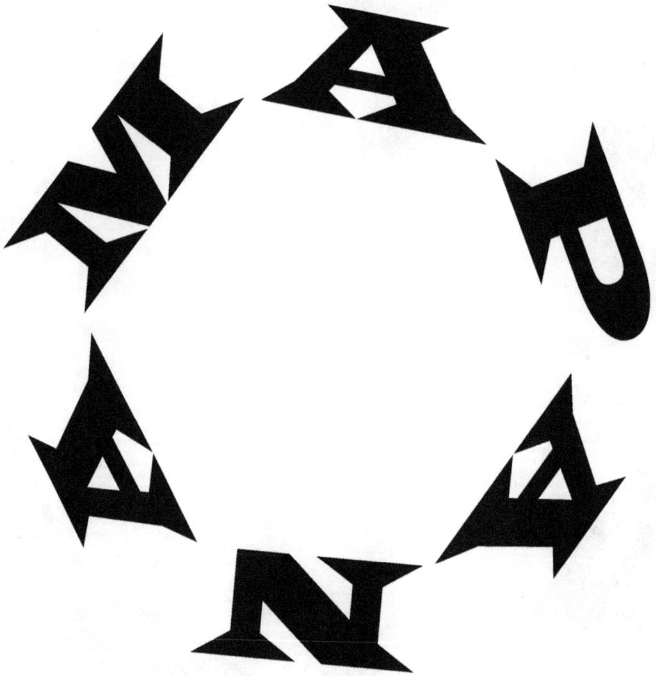
MAPANA

POVERTY

RILESTER

92

U L A P E N I N S

93

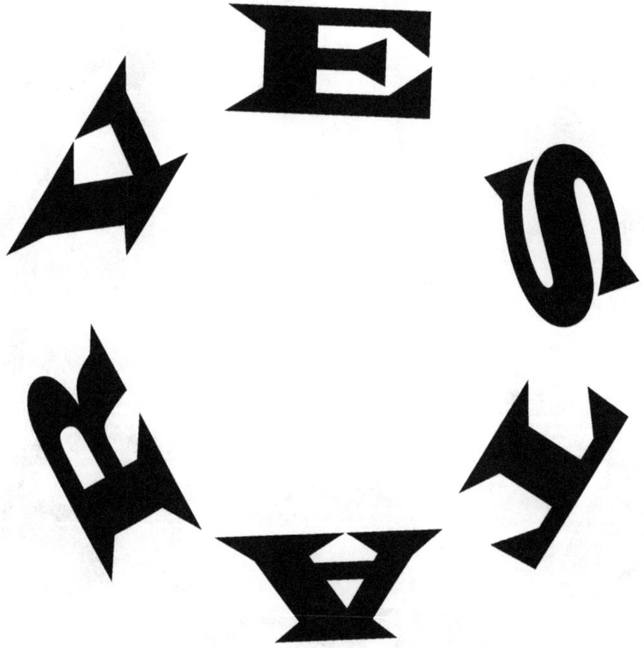
E
S
T
A
R
V

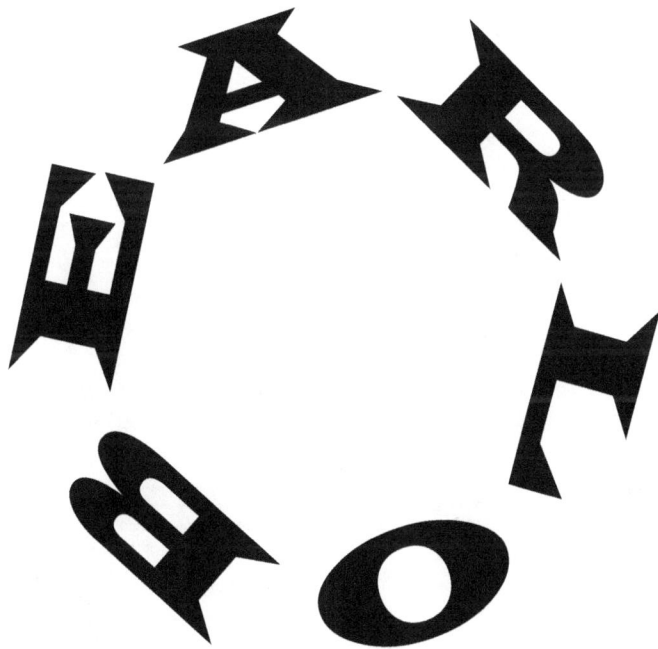

ARCHITECTURE

96

REFRAME

ENTREPRISE

S T R R I P E E

EXTRAPOLATE

100

STORES

ANESTHETIC

102

STABLE

TESTRIA

ESSENTIAL

INCANDESCENT

PATINA

SIDE OGRAPHISM

108

STILL ILLUSION

109

MUSHIPPOPOTAMUS

110

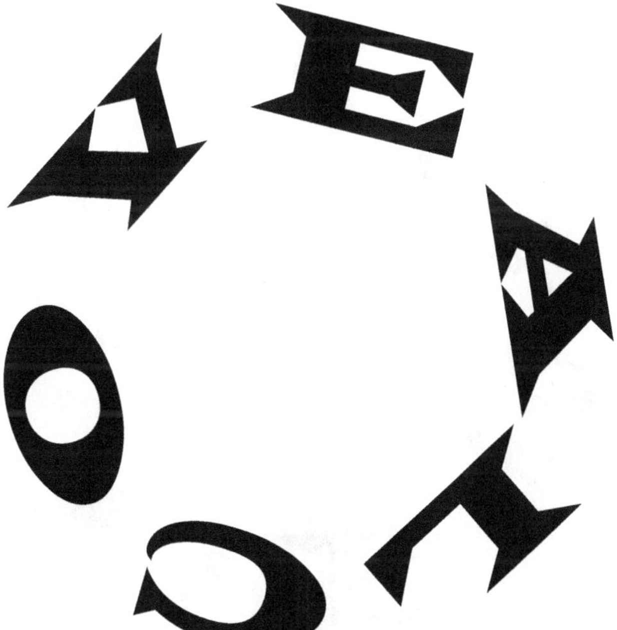

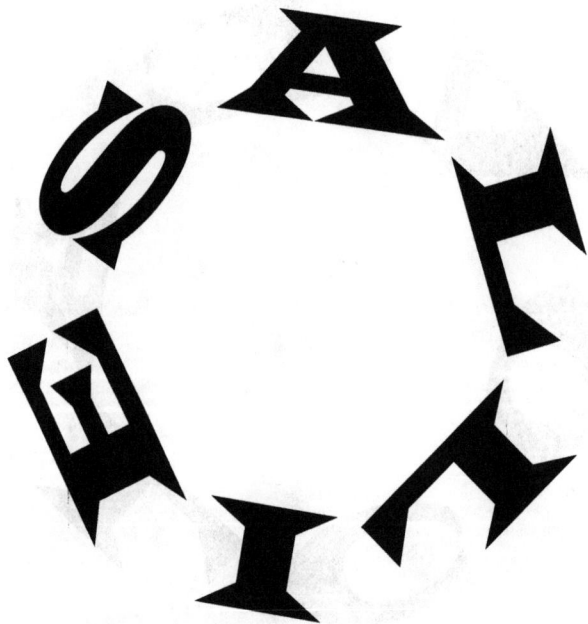

A N I T Y M P

113

TEMPERAMENTE

114

THE MASTA

MASTIGMATISM

ANCESTRAL

ANECDOTAL

MINTERIM

EMPLOYMENT

120

RUBBISH

UNDRESS

WHERE ELSE

123

PLATE M

124

APPRENTICESHIP

125

ENTERPRISE

126

ONETELEPHONE

127

RATE ME

B L E Y E N E R A R

129

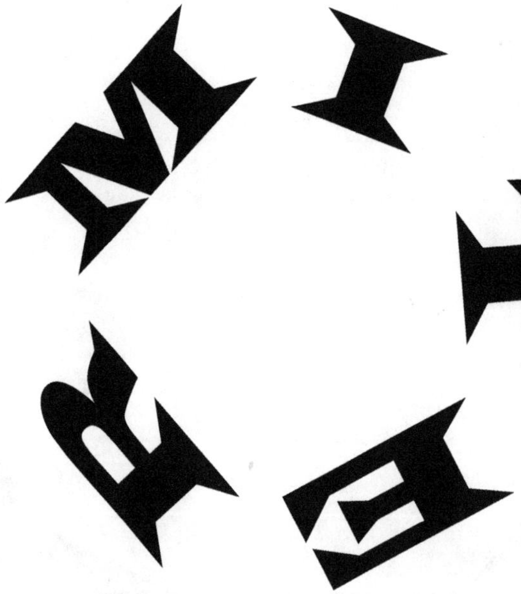
M I T E R

DOGUNDER

USTRATIVELL

OSTERMOST

OATHR

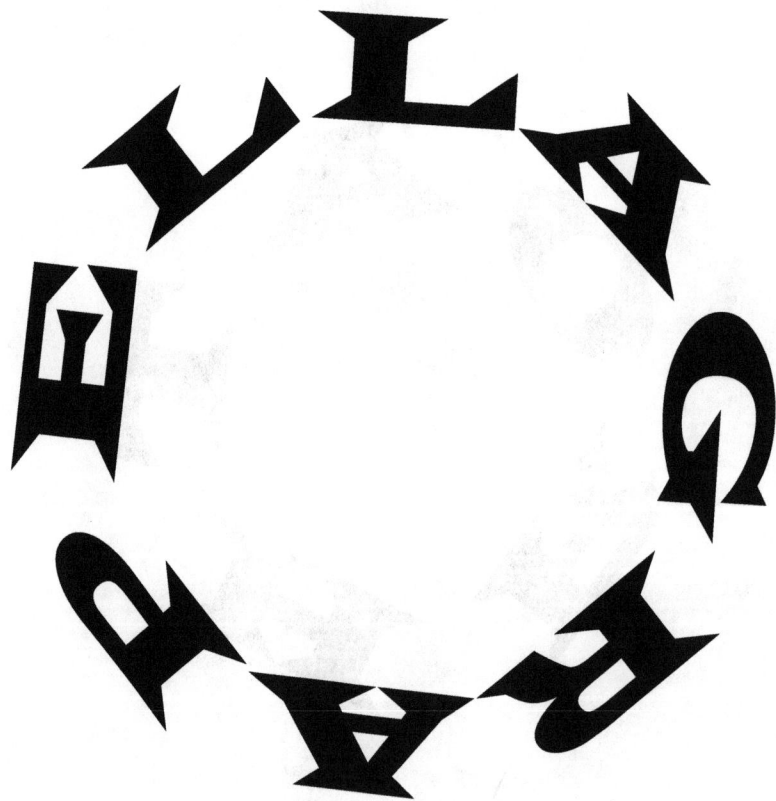

STENTRUS

ORIENTER

S T U N B E E K N O W N S

139

UNDERSTANDING

ORCHESTRA

141

SILUNCE

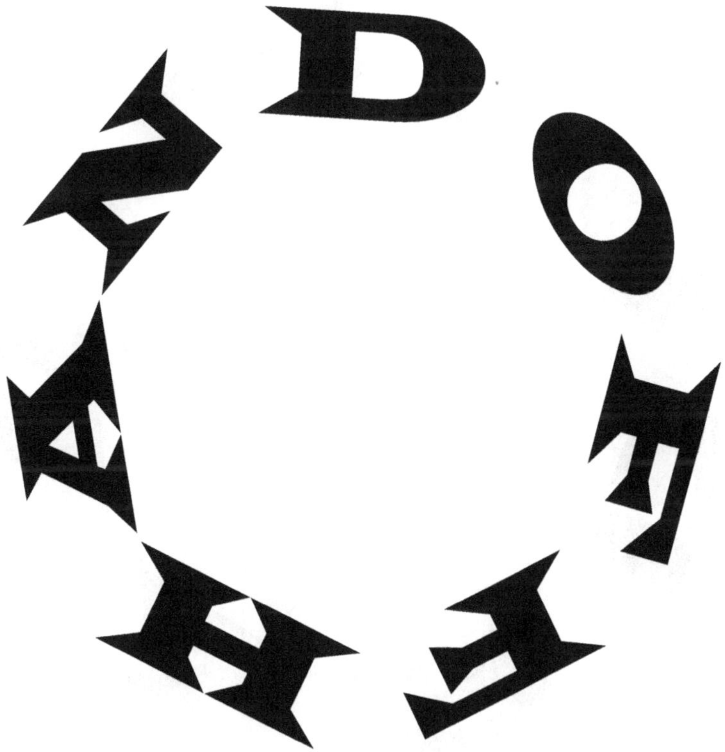
A N D O F T H

DOWNWARD

ARCHIPELAGO

THUNDER

146

PAGES PEER

150

OVERREACH

152

EARSHOLE

ISTANTHROPOLOGIST

ABANDON

EVERYWHERE

SIDE ALONGS

158

H E R B I L E A O

159

EVERGREEN

ADDRESSES

VERSATILE

162

EXTREMIST

ERASUND

DISAPPOINTED

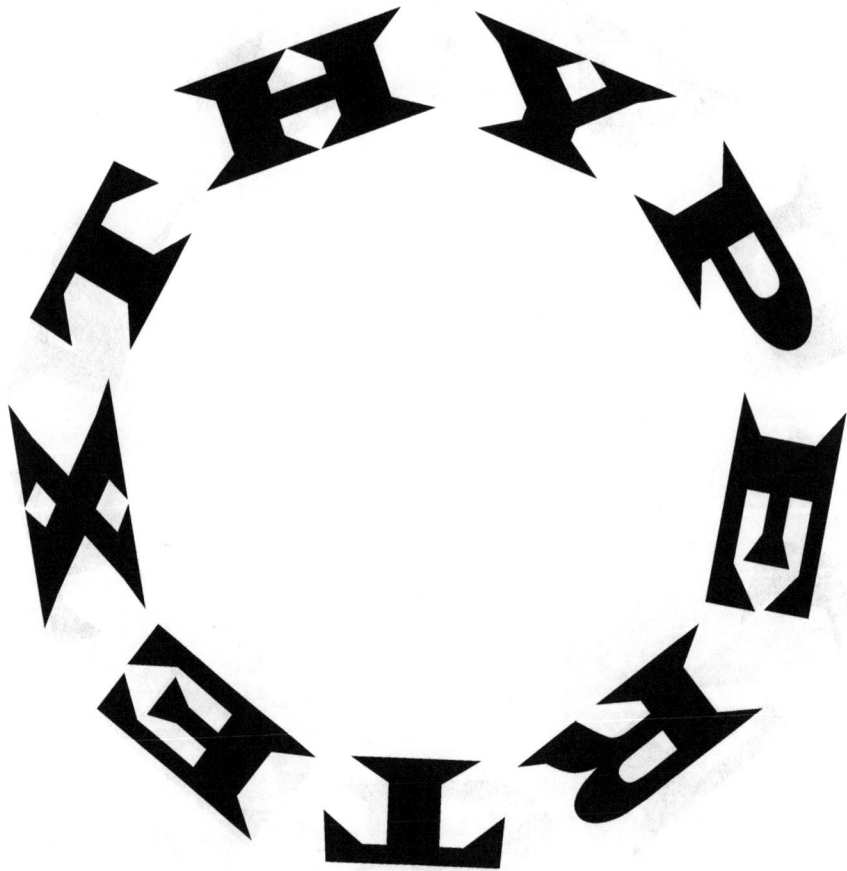

168

EXAMPLES

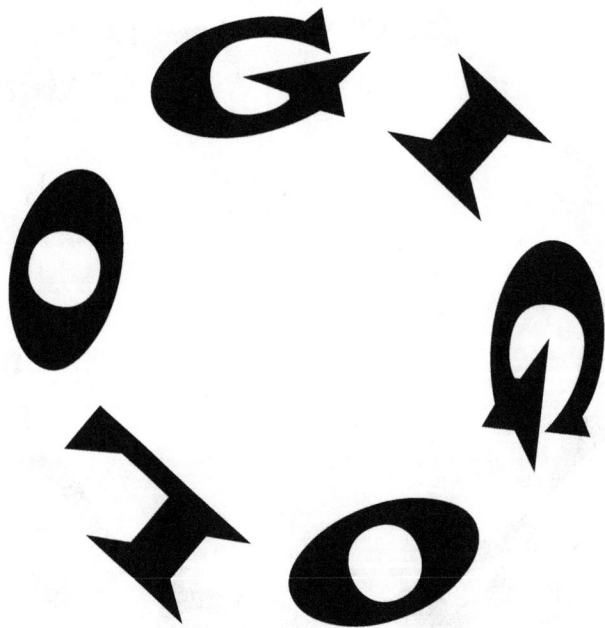

GIGOLO

170

MANTEBLLU

171

MANTON ANA

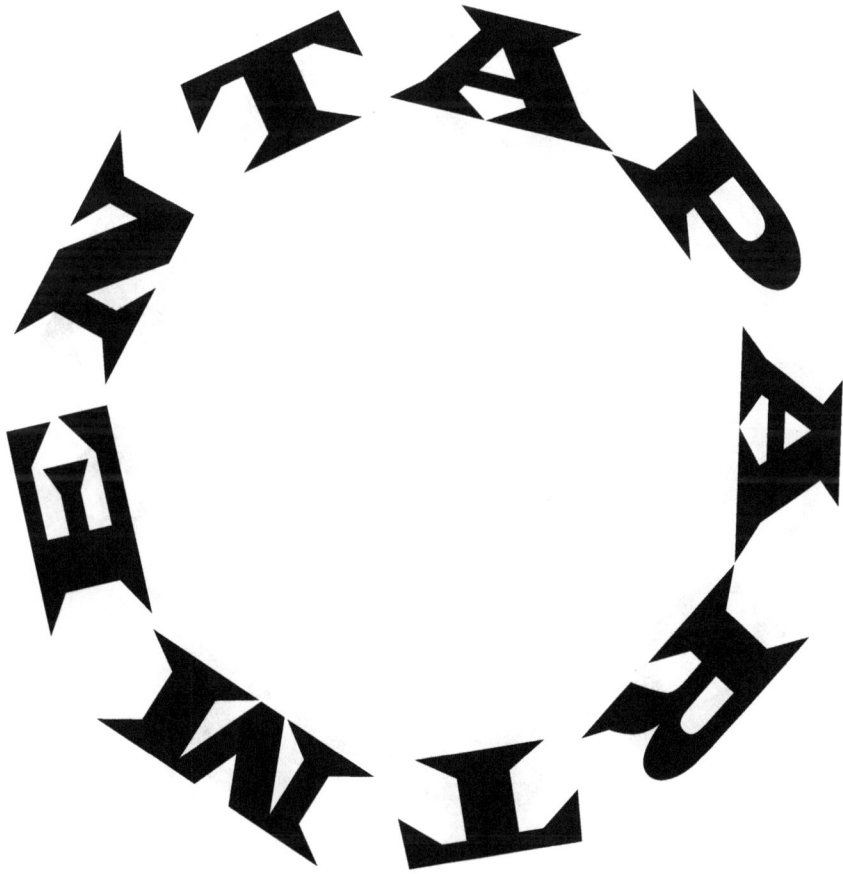

173

CATARACTS

MUSIGNORAM

MADDEN UM

176

PENTA

DOPE RATED

DESIRED

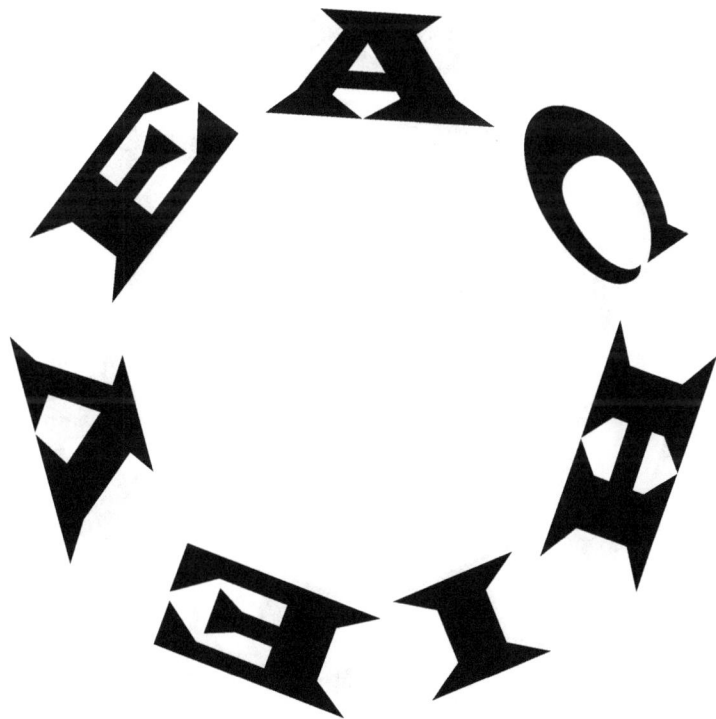

181

CLEAR OIL

182

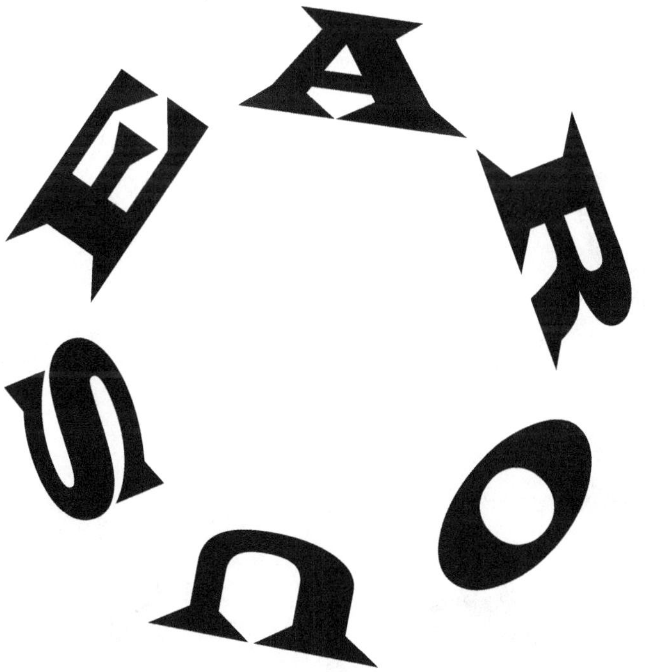
AROUSE

AUTOPILOTAUTOPILOT

SCARLETLESS

U S O N O T I R

186

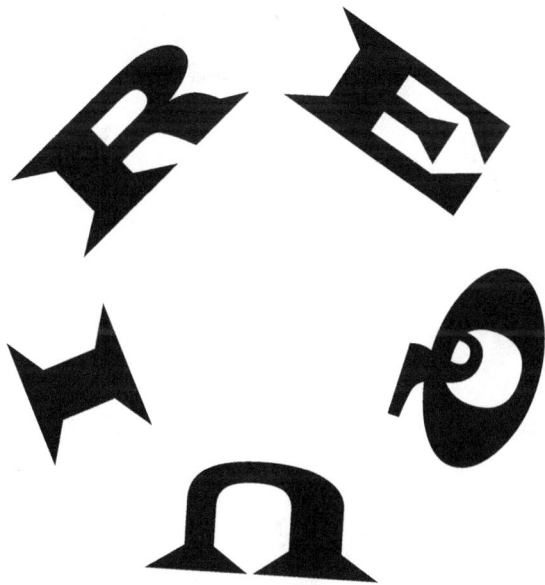

187

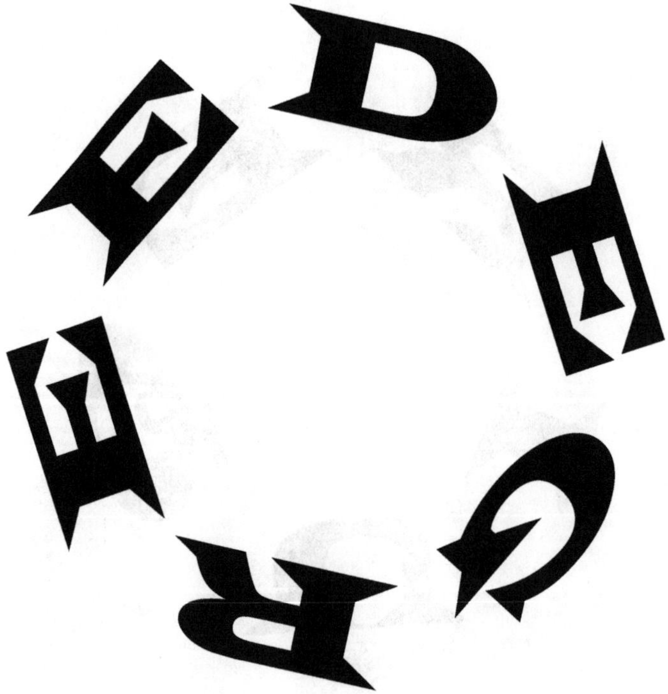
DEGREE

Individual entries on **Richard Kostelanetz**'s work in several fields appear in various editions of Readers Guide to Twentieth-Century Writers, Merriam-Webster Encyclopedia of Literature, Contemporary Poets, Contemporary Novelists, Postmodern Fiction, Webster's Dictionary of American Writers, The HarperCollins Reader's Encyclopedia of American Literature, Baker's Biographical Dictionary of Musicians, Directory of American Scholars, Who's Who in America, Who's Who in the World, Who's Who in American Art, NNDB.com, Wikipedia.com, and Britannica.com, among other distinguished directories. Otherwise, he survives in New York, where he was born, unemployed and thus overworked.

www.ingramcontent.com/pod-product-compliance
Lightning Source LLC
Chambersburg PA
CBHW081417090426
42738CB00017B/3393